10/10

BLAZERS

SHARK ZONE

GREAT WHITE SHARK

by Jody Sullivan Rake

Reading Consultant:
Barbara J. Fox
Reading Specialist
North Carolina State University

Content Consultant:
Deborah Nuzzolo
Education Manager
SeaWorld, San Diego

CAPSTONE PRESS
a capstone imprint

Blazers is published by Capstone Press,
151 Good Counsel Drive, P.O. Box 669, Mankato, Minnesota 56002.
www.capstonepub.com

Books published by Capstone Press are manufactured with paper
containing at least 10 percent post-consumer waste.

Library of Congress Cataloging-in-Publication Data
Rake, Jody Sullivan.
  Great white shark / by Jody Sullivan Rake.
    p. cm.—(Blazers. Shark zone.)
  Includes bibliographical references and index.
  Summary: "Describes the great white shark, including physical features, habitat, hunting,
and role in the ecosystem"—Provided by publisher.
  ISBN 978-1-4296-5013-7 (library binding)
  1. White shark—Juvenile literature. I. Title. II. Series.

QL638.95.L3R35 2011
597.3'3—dc22   2010002270

Editorial Credits
Lori Shores, editor; Juliette Peters, designer; Kelly Garvin, media researcher;
  Laura Manthe, production specialist

Photo Credits
Dreamstime/Willtu, 21
Jeff Rotman, 6, 7, 12, 28–29
Seapics/Amos Nachoum, 5; C & M Fallows, 15, 25; David B. Fleetham, 9, 16, 18–19; Doug
  Perrine, 22–23; Gary Bell, 17; Michael Patrick O'Neill, 11; Nigel Marsh, 26–27; Phillip
  Colla, cover
Shutterstock/artida; Eky Chan; Giuseppe_R, design elements

Essential content terms are **bold** and are defined on the page where they first appear.

TABLE OF CONTENTS

CHAPTER 1

THE KING OF SHARKS

A huge predator lurks in the cool waters near a rocky shore. Its missile-shaped body glides through the water. A powerful half-moon tail fin pushes it forward silently.

predator—an animal that hunts other animals for food

Suddenly a large gray fin rises above the water. The fin is a familiar warning as it slices through the waves. A great white shark is on the prowl.

Great white sharks are named for their bright white underbellies. Their backsides are dark gray.

TWO TONS OF TERROR

The great white shark is the world's largest hunting fish. It can grow 21 feet (6.4 meters) long. The largest great whites weigh about 4,000 pounds (1,814 kilograms).

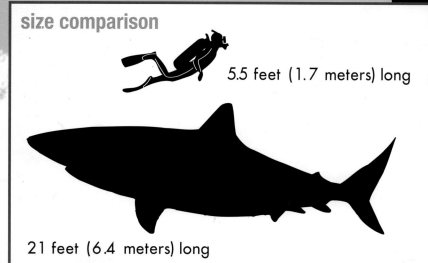

size comparison

5.5 feet (1.7 meters) long

21 feet (6.4 meters) long

The great white is a strong swimmer. **Pectoral** fins and a broad **dorsal** fin give the shark balance in the water. A powerful tail fin pushes the shark up to 25 miles (40 kilometers) per hour.

pectoral fin—the hard, flat body part on either side of a shark

dorsal fin—the hard, flat body part that sticks up from a shark's back

dorsal fin

pectoral fins

The great white's deadliest weapon is its teeth. Large, sharp, and jagged teeth hold and slice prey.

SHARK FACT

Great whites have many rows of teeth. When they lose a tooth, another moves up to replace it.

prey—an animal hunted by another animal for food

Great whites hunt many kinds of prey. They eat fish, sea otters, and dolphins. But they hunt mainly fatty seals and sea lions.

SHARK FACT

Great whites can leap clear out of the water when they attack.

Great whites use **instinct** and sharp senses to hunt. They smell blood up to 3 miles (4.8 kilometers) away. **Sense organs** in their skin help find prey.

instinct—behavior that an animal knows at birth and does not have to learn

sense organ—a body part that sends messages to the brain

Close-up of Skin

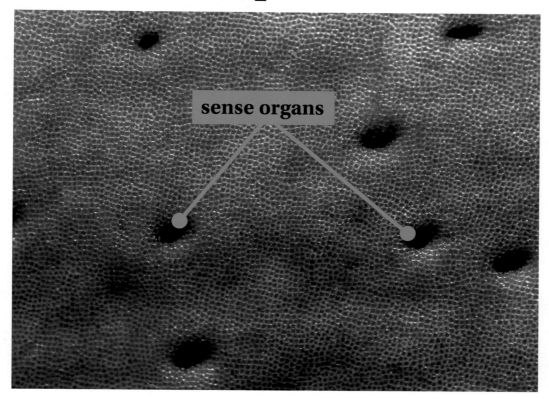

sense organs

SHARK FACT

The organs on a great white's sides sense movement. The organs on its snout sense prey.

Great whites usually swim and hunt alone. Several great whites may hunt in one place when prey is in large supply. After a large meal, a great white may go a month before hunting again.

CHAPTER 3

COASTAL LIVING

Great white sharks live in all the world's oceans except in **polar** areas. They are most common in **temperate** waters. Great whites are often seen off the coasts of California, Australia, and South Africa.

polar—having to do with the icy regions around the North or South Pole

temperate—not very hot and not very cold

Great White Range

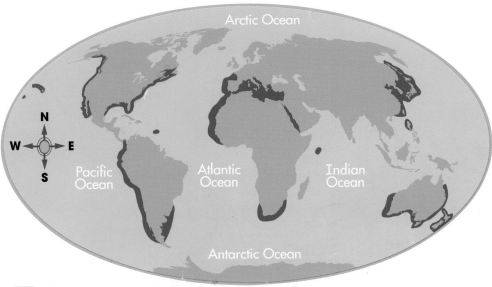

Arctic Ocean

N
W E
S

Pacific
Ocean

Atlantic
Ocean

Indian
Ocean

Antarctic Ocean

where great white sharks live

Ocean **ecosystems** need great white sharks. Great whites keep animal populations balanced. Without these sharks, seal and sea lion populations would grow too large.

ecosystem—a group of animals and plants that work together with their surroundings

CHAPTER 4

FRIGHTFULLY AMAZING

Great white sharks amaze and frighten people. But they rarely attack humans. Only one or two people are attacked each year. Most shark attack victims survive.

SHARK FACT

Scientists believe the way surfers look in the water may attract great whites. From below, surfers look like seals or sea lions.

Human activity has made great whites **endangered** animals. Many great whites become tangled in fishing nets. People also catch great whites as trophies.

endangered—at risk of dying out

SHARK FACT

Scientists don't how many great whites swim the oceans. But they do know the great white population is decreasing in some areas.

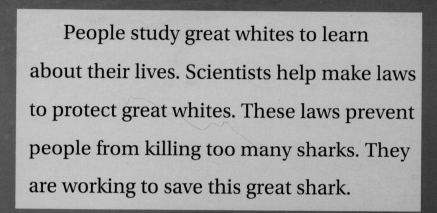

People study great whites to learn about their lives. Scientists help make laws to protect great whites. These laws prevent people from killing too many sharks. They are working to save this great shark.

Glossary

dorsal fin (DOR-suhl FIN)—the hard, flat body part that sticks up from a shark's back

ecosystem (EE-koh-sis-tuhm)—a group of animals and plants that work together with their surroundings

endangered (in-DAYN-juhrd)—at risk of dying out

instinct (IN-stingkt)—behavior that an animal knows at birth and does not have to learn

pectoral fin (PEK-tor-uhl FIN)—the hard, flat body part on either side of a shark

polar (POH-lur)—having to do with the icy regions around the North or South Pole

predator (PRED-uh-tur)—an animal that hunts other animals for food

prey (PRAY)—an animal hunted by another animal for food

sense organ (SENSS OR-guhn)—a body part that sends messages to the brain

temperate (TEM-pur-it)—an area that has neither very high nor very low temperatures

Read More

Bredeson, Carmen. *Great White Sharks Up Close.* Zoom in on Animals! Berkeley Heights, N.J.: Enslow Elementary, 2006.

Randolph, Joanne. *The Great White Shark: King of the Ocean.* Sharks: Hunters of the Deep. New York: PowerKids Press, 2007.

Riehecky, Janet. *Great White Sharks: On the Hunt.* Killer Animals. Mankato, Minn.: Capstone Press, 2009.

Smith, Miranda. *Sharks.* Kingfisher Knowledge. New York: Kingfisher, 2008.

Internet Sites

FactHound offers a safe, fun way to find Internet sites related to this book. All of the sites on FactHound have been researched by our staff.

Here's all you do:

Visit *www.facthound.com*

FactHound will fetch the best sites for you!

Index